duction

f the work of this world is performed not by the great or the
t by hordes of ordinary people. In the same way most of the
e railway was performed by ordinary locomotives. No class of
e has been a more typical work horse than the 2-6-0 type. On the
type was used on all classes of traffic from the humble loose-
eight to all but the fastest of passenger trains. For many years
ss engines hauled the fastest fitted freight trains in the country on
s.

e Messrs Clay and Cliffe in their introduction to The LNER 2-6-0
rst published in 1978. Numbering some 344 locomotives
d between 1912 and 1950, the five classes that represented the
-0s are amongst the unsung heroes of Britain s steam locomotive
book is designed to pay tribute to these locomotives and to
he work they undertook during their careers.

ey 'K1' class
0 locomotives of the 2-6-0 wheel arrangement built for the Great
Railway also represented the first design to emerge from
Works following the appointment of Nigel Gresley to the post of
hanical Engineer. The first of the H2 class, as they were
by the GNR, was built at Doncaster in 1912, the other nine
in 1913. The type was fitted with a relatively small diameter

boiler with a pressure of 170psi. The first was fitted with 3ft 8in-diameter
wheel on the pony truck, but the later nine had this reduced to 3ft 2in.
Along with Gresley s later 2-6-0 designs, they were nicknamed Ragtimers
on account of their ride, but despite this they proved themselves effective
and hard-working locomotives, initially on fast freight services between
London and Peterborough; they later saw service on secondary passenger
trains. Numbered 1630-9 by the GNR, they became Nos 4630-9 following
the Grouping, being given the LNER classification K1 ; however, by this
time Gresley had started the process of fitting them with larger boilers, thus
effectively converting them to the later K2 design. The first locomotive
to be fitted with a larger boiler was so treated in June 1920 and the last in
July 1937.

The Gresley 'K2' class

Based upon experience with the K1 class, the K2 class (GNR Class H3)
was introduced in 1913 but was fitted with a larger 5ft 6in diameter
compared to 4ft 9in boiler. A total of 65 were built Nos 1640-59 by
Doncaster Works between 1913 and 1916, Nos 1660 79 by North British in
1918 and Nos 1680-1704 by Kitson & Co in 1920/1. The first modification
occurred in 1918 with the delivery of No 1660, the first to be fitted from
new with outside steam pipes, following which the earlier locomotives
were modified.

er: Having arrived with the 5.42pm service from Mallaig,
2012 backs out of Fort William station with a van on 22 May
Mensing

er: 'K3' No 61868 south of Retford with a northbound freight
notive was constructed at Darlington Works in October 1925
No 229, becoming No 1868 at the time of the 1946
ing. The bridge in the background carried the old A1 in the
re the construction of the new main road to the west of the
ek Penney

page: On 12 September 1959, towards the end of the very
mer that marked that year, March-allocated 'K1' No 62051
thwards at Bishops Stortford with an up freight. R. C. Riley

First published 2004

ISBN 0 7110 3061 8

Published by Ian Allan Publishing

an imprint of Ian Allan Publishing Ltd, Hersham, Surrey KT12 4RG.
Printed by Ian Allan Printing Ltd, Hersham, Surrey KT12 4RG.

Code: 0409/B

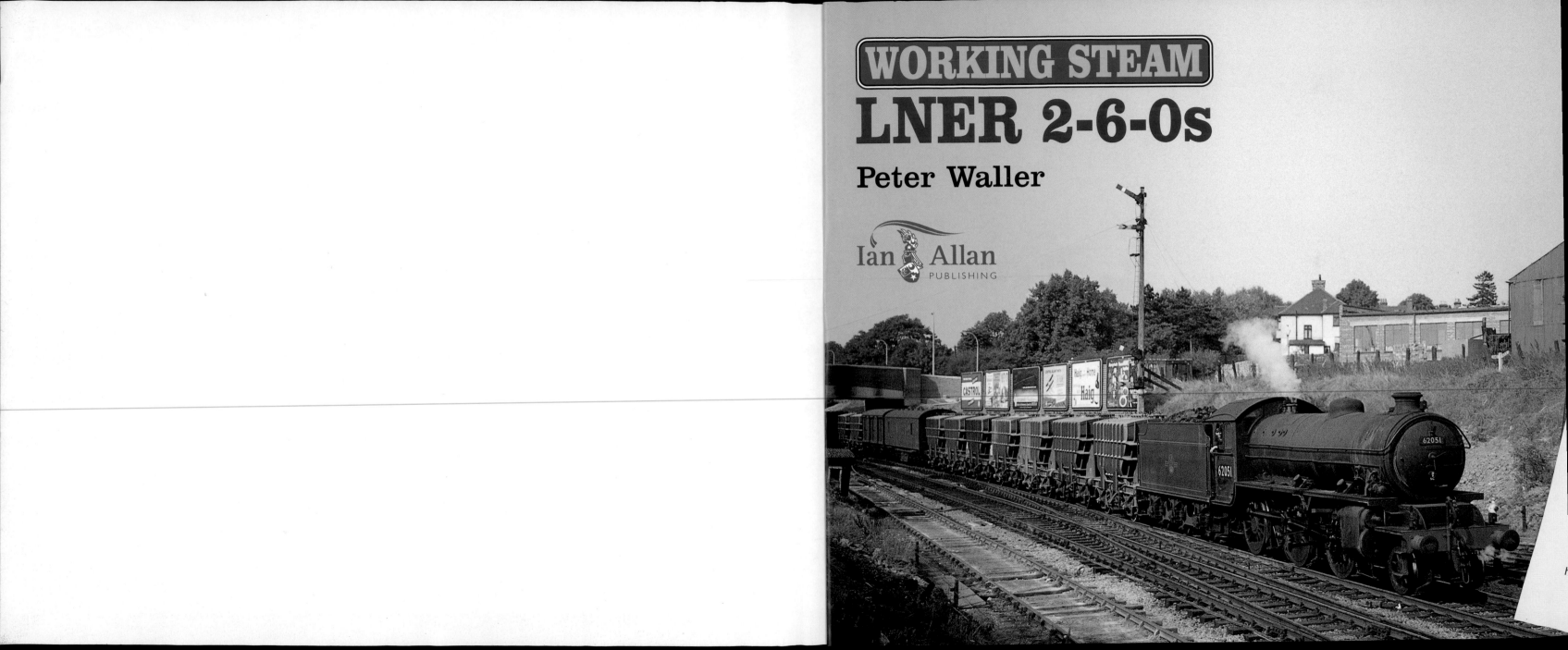

WORKING STEAM
LNER 2-6-0s

Peter Waller

Ian Allan
PUBLISHING

Left: Regrettably none of Gresley's small-boilered GNR 'H2' class seems to have survived long enough to be recorded in colour in original form. Nevertheless, the fifth example to be built — No 1634, constructed at Doncaster Works in February 1913 — is depicted here to illustrate the type as built. This locomotive would be renumbered 4634 following the Grouping and rebuilt as a 'K2' in June 1931. Renumbered again in 1946 as 1724, it was to become BR No 61724 upon Nationalisation, remaining in service until January 1958.
Ian Allan Library

was such that after the Grouping, as ... ed to extend their route availability. ... loading gauge than had the other ... ficant modifications were made in ... ble of operating away from the GNR. ... shorter chimneys and domes and the ... ab roof to the top of the firebox. For the ... land between 1925 and 1932 further ... f deeper ashpans and, in order to ... s on the harsh West Highland line, low-

e earlier small-boilered 'K1' class, a total ... R to BR in 1948. Spread over much of ... continued to give sterling service until the ... d them surplus. In Scotland they were ... West Highland duties by ex-LMS 'Black ... ferred to unfamiliar haunts in northeast ... September 1955, and only two survived ... England and No 61756 at King's Cross,

withdrawn in May and June respectively although both were to be used for steam-heating duties at King's Cross shed until its closure in June 1963.

The Gresley 'K3' class
Whilst Gresley's first 2-6-0 designs for the GNR had both been two-cylinder, in 1920 the first of his new three-cylinder design the K3 (GNR Class H4) appeared. Some 193 of the class would be built, between 1920 and 1937, construction being split between Doncaster and Darlington Works and three outside contractors (Armstrong Whitworth, North British and Robert Stephenson & Hawthorn). The first locomotive, No 1000, was also the first in Britain to be constructed with a 6ft-diameter boiler; this, combined with a slight increase in boiler pressure (to 180psi), resulted in a significant increase in tractive effort: the 'K3' class represented an increase of almost 50% over the power achieved by both the 'K1' and 'K2' classes.

Apart from the boiler, the major innovation with the 'K3' class was the design of the valve-gear, in which Gresley had been influenced by H. Holcroft of the South Eastern & Chatham Railway. When first built the locomotives were used on fast goods services and earned the nickname

Jazzers as a result of their running at speed. A coal strike in 1921 saw the early examples of the class used on passenger services between London and Doncaster, where, in order to conserve coal, trains were often combined to include up to 19 carriages with a gross weight of more than 600 tons. Despite this, the locomotives proved capable of maintaining the scheduled 50mph for the trip.

Further examples of the class were constructed after the Grouping, but with modified cab and chimney in order to meet the more restricted loading gauge of the ex-NER network. Construction of the class continued until 1937, when the last emerged from Darlington Works. However, whilst the locomotives were undoubtedly successful and powerful, their weight restricted their route availability.

Used on both passenger and freight services, from 1948 onwards the locomotives were painted in BR mixed-traffic livery of lined black (having previously been plain black) with the exception of apple-green No 1935, which emerged from Doncaster in 1947. All were still in service at the start of 1957, but thereafter withdrawals were rapid, and the class became extinct with the withdrawal of No 61985 in December 1962. None was to survive into preservation.

The Gresley 'K4' class
Constituting what was numerically the smallest of the LNER 2-6-0 classes, the six three-cylinder K4s were built specifically for service on the West Highland line and were thus graced with names redolent of that part of Scotland. The need for more powerful motive power over the line to Fort William and Mallaig resulted in Gresley initially contemplating a 2-8-0 design, but this was soon rejected in favour of the 2-6-0. With the existing K3 class rejected due to weight restrictions, Gresley endeavoured to produce the most powerful 2-6-0 possible within existing weight limits. Combining a shortened B17 boiler with standard K3 cylinders at 180psi and 5ft 2in driving wheels, the K4 design achieved a tractive effort of 32,940lb; this was later increased to 36,598lb when the boiler pressure was increased to 200psi. The result was to allow the new class to haul West Highland-line trains which were more than a third heavier than those permitted for the K2 class. However, a consequence of the small driving wheels was that the class could achieve little more than 60mph on level track.

Constructed at Darlington Works between 1937 and 1939, the K4s were to be based on the West Highland line for some 20 years. Originally numbered 3441-6, they were renumbered 1993-8 in 1946. By this date,

however, No 3445 MacCailin Mor had been rebuilt to a design of Edward Thompson; as such it formed the prototype for the later K1 class. Of the five remaining locomotives, all were to be transferred away from the West Highland line in the twilight of their careers, being based until withdrawal in Fife. One No 3442 The Great Marquess survives in preservation, having been acquired on withdrawal by Viscount Garnock.

The Thompson 'K5' class
A total of 193 members of the three-cylinder K3 class were built; of these 192 passed to BR in 1948. The exception was No 1863, which as LNER No 206 was converted in June 1945 from a three-cylinder to two-cylinder design. As rebuilt the locomotive was fitted with a Diagram 96A 225psi boiler. The result of the modification was a slight reduction in tractive effort, from the 30,030lb of the original three-cylinder design to 29,250lb. Allocated to the ex-GE section for most of its career, as a non-standard locomotive No 61863 (as it subsequently became) was a relatively early casualty, being withdrawn in June 1960.

The Thompson 'K1/1' class
In 1945 Edward Thompson took K4 No 3445, then due a heavy overhaul, and modified it as the basis of a planned new class of two-cylinder 2-6-0s designed to replace the Gresley-designed J38 and J39 0-6-0s. Fitted with a B1 -type boiler, an O1 -type pony truck and other standard parts, the locomotive continued to be based largely in Scotland after conversion. However, whilst the two-cylinder design resulted in a locomotive that was easier to maintain, the reduction in tractive effort (by about 6,500lb) made it less suitable for operation on the West Highland line. Despite this, as No 61997 it remained allocated to Fort William until withdrawal in 1961.

The Peppercorn 'K1' class
Although no more conversions of existing 2-6-0 designs were undertaken, the Thompson K1/1 design nevertheless formed the basis of the last new class of LNER 2-6-0 design the Peppercorn K1 of which 70 were constructed by North British, after Nationalisation, between May 1949 and March 1950. When delivered the locomotives spent some time at Eastfield for running-in prior to despatch to the North Eastern and Eastern regions; 40 were allocated initially to the NER and 30 to the ER. The first 10 allocated to the ER, Nos 62011-20, were sent to Gorton, Manchester, but their time there was limited, and they were soon sent southwards, to March. The first K1s allocated officially to Scotland were transferred in 1952,

and, as examples were made redundant from the ER as a result of dieselisation, from 1959 the class reappeared on the ex-GC section, allocated for example to Frodingham and Retford. Perceived as a smaller version of the B1 4-6-0, the K1 acquired the nickname Baby Bongo .

As with so many other steam locomotives constructed after World War 2, the K1s were to be withdrawn prematurely, all 70 succumbing between December 1962 and December 1967. The last example to be withdrawn, No 62005, would ultimately be preserved, although at one stage its survival was open to doubt, as it was retained initially to provide a possible spare boiler for the preserved No 3442 The Great Marquess; for a brief period after withdrawal it was also used to provide steam heating for an ICI plant at Port Clarence. Today the locomotive is preserved on the North Yorkshire Moors Railway.

Acknowledgements
I am grateful to the following for their assistance in the compilation of this book: Roy Hobbs, Michael Mensing, Derek Penney, Dick Riley, Geoff Rixon, Brian Stephenson and Ron White. Information for the introduction and captions has been gathered from a variety of sources. However, a book of this nature can provide only a brief introduction to the classes of locomotives concerned, and readers seeking a detailed account are recommended to peruse the following books and magazines:

Gresley Locomotives by Brian Haresnape (Ian Allan, 1981)
Locomotives Illustrated 53: Gresley Three-cylinder 2-6-0s (Ian Allan, 1987)
Locomotives Illustrated 67: Gresley Two-cylinder 2-6-0s (Ian Allan, 1989)
Locomotives of the LNER, Part 6A: Tender Engines — Classes J38 to K5 (RCTS, 1982)
The LNER 2-6-0 Classes by J. F. Clay and J. Cliffe (Ian Allan, 1978)
Thompson and Peppercorn — Locomotive Engineers by Col H. C. B. Rogers (Ian Allan, 1979)
What Happened to Steam, Volume 24: The ER 2-6-0s by P. B. Hands (published by the author, 1982)
Yeadon's Register of LNER Locomotives, Vol 8: Gresley K3 and K4 Classes (Challenger, 1995)
Yeadon's Register of LNER Locomotives, Vol 18: Gresley K1 and K2, Thompson K1/1 and Peppercorn K1 (Challenger, 2000)

It's July 1959, and 'K4' No 61996 *Lord of the Isles* makes a dramatic entrance into North Queensferry with a southbound service towards Edinburgh across the Forth Bridge. Like No 61993, this locomotive had been transferred to Thornton Junction in April 1959, where it would survive until withdrawal in October 1961.
C. J. B. Sanderson/ Colour-Rail (Sc793)

Great Eastern

Below: The last 2-6-0 constructed to an LNER design, Peppercorn 'K1' No 62070, at Bethnal Green with an ECS working on 28 February 1959. At this date the locomotive was allocated to March but would be transferred to Stratford the following June. *R. C. Riley*

Right: March-allocated 'K1' No 62018 awaits its next duty at Stratford shed on 18 August 1959. The locomotive would remain allocated to March until transferred to Frodingham in early January 1960. *K. L. Cook/Rail Archive Stephenson*

Left: Also pictured at Stratford but on 7 May 1961, towards the end of its working life on the ex-GE section, 'K1' No 62040 was allocated to March until October 1961 and then transferred to Retford. A final transfer, in November 1962, saw it reallocated to Doncaster, from where it was withdrawn in January 1965.
K. L. Cook/Rail Archive Stephenson

Below: March-based 'K1' No 62013 heads past Copper Mill Junction signalbox, near Stratford, with an up extra in September 1955. This particular locomotive was allocated to Stratford shed for only a relatively brief period, between December 1958 and January 1960, after which it was allocated to Frodingham until withdrawal in October 1963. It was one of the first of the class to be taken out of service, being one of only nine withdrawn that year. *Colour-Rail (BRE1399)*

Above: Captured heading northeastwards from Witham Junction, 'K3/2' No 61849, then allocated to Stratford, provides the motive power for the 9.46am service from London Liverpool Street to Harwich on 2 August 1958. Witham was the junction for the line westwards to Braintree, which remains open, and that eastwards to Maldon East & Heybridge, which would close to passengers on 7 September 1964 and to freight on 18 April 1966. *K. L. Cook/ Rail Archive Stephenson*

Right: Immaculate 'K3' No 61953 heads south towards the up distant signal at Oulton with an up Saturday extra in September 1958. A Norwich-allocated locomotive at this date, it would be transferred via Colwick and New England to its final shed, Doncaster, in September 1961. *E. Algar/Colour-Rail (BRE1401)*

Above: Seen just south of Colchester, Norwich-allocated 'K3/2' No 61908 heads southwards with the 11.50am service from Yarmouth South to London Liverpool Street on 5 September 1959.
K. L. Cook/Rail Archive Stephenson

Right: On the same day, but slightly earlier, the photographer witnessed another 2-6-0 on an up passenger working when he recorded March-allocated 'K1' No 62051 heading an express towards Liverpool Street. It is interesting to note that in this view of the slight up gradient towards Marks Tey the fireman is working hard, whereas in the previous photograph No 61908 is blowing off steam.
K. L. Cook/Rail Archive Stephenson

Lowestoft Central-allocated 'K3' No 61949 pictured at Coke Ovens Junction, Lowestoft, with a mixed freight on 22 May 1957. This locomotive would remain allocated to Lowestoft until transferred to Norwich in February the following year. *R. C. Riley*

It's the summer of 1957 — July, to be precise — as, under a clear blue sky, Lowestoft-allocated 'K3/2' No 61957, in immaculate external condition, departs from Lowestoft with the up 'Holiday Camps Express'. *E. Algar/Colour-Rail (BRE1402)*

Above: In August 1957, at the height of the summer season, 'K3' No 61867 is pictured near Belton, to the south of Great Yarmouth, with an up summer Saturday relief. Note the use of discs rather than headlamps. *E. Algar/Colour-Rail (BRE1486)*

Right: Looking superb in lined black, March-allocated 'K3' No 61810 awaits departure from Norwich on 31 May 1960. As LNER No 17 this locomotive was the first of the class to be built after the Grouping, in August 1924, and also the first to be built at Darlington Works. Renumbered 1810 in 1946, the locomotive was to survive until August 1962, by which date it had departed the ex-GE section for the ex-GC lines. *R. C. Riley*

Above: Heading due south on 6 September 1958, March-allocated 'K1' No 62055 is pictured at Cheshunt with a service for Liverpool Street. At this point the area to the east of the railway is dominated by the canalised Lea Navigation and the River Lea; although the backdrop looks sylvan, the reality is that Cheshunt was just outside the Greater London area and, from this point onwards, passengers would see a virtually unending built-up area.
K. L. Cook/Rail Archive Stephenson

Right: The evening sun catches the side of 'K3' No 61834, seen taking water at the north end of Cambridge station on 16 June 1960. At this date allocated, appropriately, to Cambridge (31A) shed, the locomotive would be transferred in October the following year to March, from where it would be withdrawn in May 1962. *R. C. Riley*

Left: Seen at March, in January 1959, 'K3/2' No 61862 looks in fine external condition as the sun catches its lined-black livery. The locomotive had been transferred only the previous month from Stratford to Parkeston, where it was destined to remain until June 1960, when a final move saw it reallocated to March. *Derek Penney*

Below: Also pictured at March shed but three months later, in April 1959, is two-cylinder 'K5' No 61863. This was the sole example of its class, having been rebuilt to a design of Edward Thompson in June 1945 from a Gresley three-cylinder 'K3'. The original locomotive had been built at Darlington Works in September 1925 as LNER No 206, being renumbered 1863 in 1946. By 1959 the locomotive was allocated to Stratford, from where it would be withdrawn in June 1960. *W. Potter/Colour-Rail (BRE1487)*

Great Northern

Looking superb in ex-works condition at Doncaster in April 1958,
'K3/2' No 61826 awaits its journey to its new home shed of March
(31B). It would be reallocated two months later to Norwich.
W. Potter/Colour-Rail (BRE 1484)

Passengers wait expectantly at Kimberley in Nottinghamshire as an Ilkeston–Skegness extra hauled by 'K3' No 61856 enters the station in July 1958. One of the class to be fitted with an ex-GNR tender, No 61856 was by this date allocated to Annesley, which shed, previously coded 38B, had become 16D with the transfer of responsibility for the ex-Great Central main line to the London Midland Region in February 1958. However, the locomotive would remain in LMR ownership for a relatively short period, being transferred to Ardsley in May 1959. *Colour-Rail (BRE 1400)*

'K2' No 61771, recorded at its home shed of Boston on 23 June 1958. New in June 1921 as GNR No 1681, this locomotive was the second of 25 constructed by Kitson & Co between then and September 1921. Initially renumbered 4681 following the Grouping, it became No 1771 under the LNER's 1946 renumbering scheme. Transferred to Boston (40F) in March 1958, it was to remain based here for a relatively short period before a further transfer exactly a year later saw it migrate to Immingham. A final transfer, in September 1960, involved a return to Colwick (where it had been allocated for much of the early 1950s) for its last three months. *K. L. Cook/Rail Archive Stephenson*

Also present at Boston on the same occasion was sister 'K2' No 61766. This was one of 20 examples built by North British (Works No 21987 of August 1918) between June and August 1918. Originally GNR No 1676, it became No 4676 following the Grouping and 1766 in 1946. Boston was its home shed until February 1959, when it was transferred to Immingham, moving thence in June 1960 to Colwick, from where it would be withdrawn in January 1961.
K. L. Cook/Rail Archive Stephenson

The first of the 'K3' class, No 61800, at the head of a coal train at Boston on 24 June 1958. Built at Doncaster in March 1920 as GNR No 1000, it was destined to have a working life of more than 40 years, not being withdrawn (from Doncaster shed) until July 1962. The three-cylinder design adopted by Gresley for this class was based around his work the previous decade as modified at the suggestion of Harold Holcroft. The new locomotive proved successful, although the centre piston valve showed a tendency to overrun; this problem was solved by a slight modification to the radius links and a reduction in the maximum cut-off. When built the locomotive was fitted with a standard GNR cab but, like the other ex-GNR 'K3s', was to be modified to meet the slightly smaller LNER composite loading gauge and fitted with side-window cabs, all 10 being so treated between March 1939 and November 1940. *R. C. Riley*

Right: With the ex-GNR Lincoln Central station in the background, 'K3' No 61807 crosses the level crossing at Durham Ox Junction with a service to Skegness during 1955. The line to the northeast, ex-Great Central, runs towards Barnetby, but the link from this line to the ex-Midland station at St Johns is now closed, all passenger services being concentrated at Central.
No 61807 was one of the first batch of 10 'K3s' constructed by the GNR, emerging from Doncaster Works in May 1921. Originally numbered 1007, it became No 4007 at the Grouping and was renumbered 1807 as part of the 1946 renumbering scheme. Allocated to Lincoln at the time of this photograph, the locomotive would be reallocated to Immingham in January 1962.
Colour-Rail (BRE1266)

Right: 'K1' No 62033 heads along the Lincoln-avoiding line in October 1957 with a freight. Allocated at this time to March, at the southern end of the GN&GE Joint line, it would regularly have been employed on trips to Lincoln at this time. It would remain at March until December 1960, when it was reallocated to Frodingham, its final shed.
M. Longdon/Colour-Rail (BRE1482)

Above: Allocated to Colwick (its final shed, from January 1958), 'K3' No 61852 appears in reasonable condition as it heads north through Grantham with a late-evening freight in 1959. This locomotive had been built at Darlington in March 1925 and was destined to have a working life of some 36 years, surviving until July 1961. *Derek Penney*

Right: Whilst not strictly an ex-GNR location, Burton-on-Trent was reached by the GNR thanks to the latter's running powers over the North Staffordshire line from Dove Junction (on the route from Burton to Uttoxeter). Here 'K3/2' No 61896 heads southwards towards Burton with a freight at 3.59pm on 4 June 1960. The train, which probably originated from the ex-GNR Derby Friargate line, is pictured at the closed station of Streeton & Clay Mills, just to the north of Burton. *M. Mensing*

Above: 'K3' No 61950 stands in ex-works condition outside Doncaster Works in May 1959. This was one of the 20 of the class constructed by North British between August and November 1935, being completed in September as LNER No 2449. Based on the erstwhile Great Central for much of its career, it was to spend its last few months allocated to Doncaster, before withdrawal in November 1962. *D. H. Beecroft/Colour-Rail (BRE580)*

Right: Four years later, in May 1963, 'K1' No 62050 also stands in ex-works condition at Doncaster, looking superb in BR's mixed-traffic livery of lined black. The contrast in condition between the 2-6-0 and the adjacent locomotives is indicative of the fact that steam was in gradual decline. By this stage allocated to Consett, No 62050 would be transferred subsequently to Tweedmouth, Blyth and Tyne Dock before withdrawal in September 1967 (one of three examples that month) left No 62005 as the only LNER-designed 2-6-0 to remain in service. *Colour-Rail (BRE26)*

Great Central

Left: Immingham-allocated 'K3' No 61912 pictured on shed at Neasden in March 1961. By this date Neasden shed was approaching the end of its life — it would close the following year — and three years earlier had been transferred, along with the ex-GC main line, to the London Midland Region. No 61912 remained allocated at Immingham until October 1961, when it migrated to Lincoln for six months until a final transfer took it to New England, from where it was withdrawn in September 1962. However, this was not to be end of its career, as it survived in use as a stationary boiler at New England until April 1965, finally being scrapped the following month by Cashmore's of Great Bridge.
C. R. Gordon Stuart/Colour-Rail (BRE1805)

Below: Woodford Halse-allocated 'K3' No 61910 heads southwards at Beaconsfield with an up coal train on 7 May 1961. Woodford Halse shed had passed to LMR control in 1958, being recoded initially as 2G and then as 2F. No 61910 had been transferred from another ex-GC shed — Gorton, which had also passed to LMR control, in April 1960 — and would remain at Woodford Halse until withdrawal in July 1962. *K. L. Cook/Rail Archive Stephenson*

Below: An up freight passes Princes Risborough South 'box in May 1961 with Woodford Halse-allocated 'K3' No 61843 at its head. No 61843 would see out its days at Woodford Halse, eventually becoming one of 20 'K3s' withdrawn in November 1962; by the end of that year the type would be extinct in BR service. *M. R. Palmer/Colour-Rail (BRE1485)*

Right: 'K3/2' No 61907 at Colwick shed — its home since December 1959 — on 25 August 1962. By this date the locomotive was approaching the end of its career; indeed, it was destined to be withdrawn the following month. *Geoff Rixon*

Below: Colwick-allocated 'K3/2' No 61974 heads south at Heath, to the south of Chesterfield, with the 10.9am service from Sheffield Victoria to Nottingham Victoria on 29 September 1959.
Michael Mensing

Right: Having just passed through Chesterfield Central station, and with the familiar crooked spire of the town's parish church in the background, 'K3' No 61854 heads southeast towards Arkwright in 1961. The locomotive is fitted with a GNR tender, as were a number of Scottish-allocated 'K3s'. Transferred to the North Eastern Region at Hull Dairycoates in February 1957, it moved to Tweedmouth before returning to Dairycoates in September 1961 for its final year of service, withdrawal coming in October 1962.
Trainslides/Colour-Rail (BRE1614)

It's August 1958, and 'K3' No 61974 is heading westwards near Ollerton with a return excursion from Bridlington to Chesterfield. Constructed as LNER No 3814 at Darlington in November 1936, by the date of this photograph the locomotive was allocated to Colwick; it would remain based on the ex-GC main line until a final transfer, in December 1960, saw it end its days at another ex-GC shed — Immingham. *G. Warnes/Colour-Rail (BRE1719)*

Pictured approaching Retford from the east on the line from Lincoln on 28 February 1959, Norwich-allocated 'K3' No 61971 heads towards Sheffield with a football special full of Norwich City fans — hence the yellow and green flags in front of the smokebox — bound for a game with Sheffield United at Bramall Lane. No 61971 was constructed at Darlington in October 1936, as LNER No 2498, one of the final batch of 24 built there between October 1936 and February 1937. Renumbered 1971 in 1946, it was allocated to Norwich for much of its later career; however, a final transfer in December 1960 saw it migrate to Colwick, from where it was withdrawn the following March. *Derek Penney*

Below: A photograph that would be impossible to replicate today, even if the three locomotives survived, sees the trio approaching the flat crossing at Retford from the Gainsborough line in July 1964. They are headed by 'K1' No 62070, the last LNER-designed 2-6-0 to be constructed, in the company of two 2-8-0s — a 'WD' and an 'O4'. By this date Doncaster-allocated No 62070 was entering the twilight of its career; it was withdrawn the following January.
W. Oliver/ Colour-Rail (BRE732)

Right: On a somewhat murky day in June 1960 — which goes to prove that the sun didn't always shine in the age of steam — 'K2/2' No 61756, only recently transferred to Colwick, stands at Nottingham Victoria station with a local for Grantham. No 61756 was one of only two members of the class to survive into 1962, being withdrawn from King's Cross shed in June of that year; it would then survive until closure of the shed, in June 1963, being used until then for steam-heating duties. *D. H. Beecroft/Colour-Rail (BRE1804)*

Underneath the 1,500V dc overhead of the Woodhead electrification scheme at Woodhouse, 'K3/2' No 61867, then allocated to Mexborough, heads a southbound passenger service during 1958.
Derek Penney

Having just passed through Brocklesby station with a westbound freight, Boston-allocated 'K2' No 61742 heads towards Barnetby. The locomotive was turned out by Doncaster Works in May 1916 as GNR No 1652. By 1962, by which time it was allocated to New England, it was one of only two examples of its class to remain in service, eventually being withdrawn in May that year, leaving No 61756 to soldier on until the following month. *A. E. Doyle/ Colour-Rail (BRE175)*

North Eastern

Below: The ex-NER branch from Harrogate (Ripley Valley Junction) to Pateley Bridge lost its passenger services on 2 April 1951 but was to remain open for freight traffic until 2 November 1964. Towards the end of the line's life, in March 1964, York-allocated 'K1' No 62046 is pictured at Ripley Valley with the goods for Pateley Bridge. *D. J. Mitchell/Colour-Rail (BRE1545)*

Right: With the vast bulk of York Minster visible in the distance, 'K2' No 61745 stands light-engine to the north of the city's station on 7 June 1958. Allocated to Boston (40F) at this date, No 61745 would be transferred to Immingham the following February. The locomotive was withdrawn in November 1960, one of 14 examples of the class to succumb that year. *R. C. Riley*

Above: Hull (Dairycoates)-allocated 'K3/3' No 61883 seen in superb external condition at the south end of York station in 1959. It would remain at Hull for the remainder of its career, being withdrawn from the shed in December 1962. *Derek Penney*

Right: Also pictured at York in 1959, but on shed rather than at the station, is 'K1' No 62042, a locomotive which had recently been transferred to Thornaby (despite the York shedplate). The contrast between the smart lined-out black of the 2-6-0 and the grime of the surrounding locomotives is all too evident. *Derek Penney*

Left: 'K1' No 62004 is seen on 25 September 1963 on the turntable at Darlington shed, where it would remain allocated for a further 15 months before a final transfer saw it migrate the relatively short distance to West Hartlepool. *Geoff Rixon*

Above: Looking as grimy as the industrial backdrop, 'K1' No 62001 arrives at its home shed of Darlington in September 1963. The first of the class to be constructed, the locomotive emerged from North British in May 1949 and had been allocated to Thornaby for four years until transferred to Darlington in April 1963. *Geoff Rixon*

Below: On 20 May 1967 the Stephenson Locomotive Society ran its 'Three Dales' railtour, starting from Stockton-on-Tees at 10.15am, at the princely sum of £2.25 (or 45s, as it was advertised at the time) per head. As planned, motive power was provided by a 'K1' 2-6-0, No 62005 being seen with the special at Richmond. The following month, according to an item in *The Railway Magazine*, this locomotive was noted in store at Tyne Dock in 'immaculate external condition and is believed to be awaiting private preservation'. Such a fate did indeed befall it upon withdrawal later in 1967, and it can now be seen on the North Yorkshire Moors Railway. Unfortunately the Richmond branch would not be so lucky and in early March 1969 was to close save for the section from Darlington to Catterick. *Colour-Rail (BRE731)*

Right: Bound for Waskerley, 'K1' No 62027 awaits departure from Consett with the joint RCTS/SLS 'North Eastern Railtour' on 28 September 1963. By this date passenger services to Consett had ceased, although the station was largely intact, and the line remained open to serve the region's various industrial sites, including the famous steelworks. *Roy Hobbs*

Below: Blaydon-allocated 'K1' No 62002 generates considerable smoke as it heads westwards at King Edward Bridge Junction, to the south of the River Tyne in Gateshead, with a freight in June 1960. The locomotive would remain allocated to Blaydon until May 1962, when it was reallocated to Consett; a further move, in June the following year, saw it reallocated to South Blyth; it was withdrawn in October 1966 from North Blyth. *Colour-Rail (BRE1398)*

Right: The Northumberland town of Alnwick is perhaps best known as the location of Alnwick Castle, home of the Duke of Northumberland, and it was the presence of this important family that guaranteed that the town's station would be built on a grand scale. A further reflection of the family's importance to the town can be seen in the background; the Percy Tenantry Column was erected in 1816 to a design by David Stephenson. Surmounted by a lion, symbol of the Percy family, it was funded by the family's tenant farmers, in gratitude for reduced rents during a period of agricultural depression. In the foreground can be seen 'K1' No 62011 awaiting departure from Alnwick station. Alnwick was effectively the terminus for two ex-NER branches — from Coldstream and from Alnmouth — but by the mid-sixties the former had been completely closed for some years. Passenger services over the Alnwick branch ceased on 29 February 1968, and freight was to succumb on 7 October. Today the station is still extant, occupied largely by a second-hand bookshop, and there are plans for reinstatement of the line to Alnmouth. *Colour-Rail (BRE416)*

On the penultimate day of steam on the Alnwick branch, 17 June 1966, 'K1' No 62021 is pictured in front of the sizeable ex-NER signalbox at the branch terminus whilst running round its train prior to making its return to Alnmouth. *Roy Hobbs*

'K1' No 62011 heads away from Alnwick station with a service for Alnmouth on 18 June 1966, the last day of steam operation on the branch. The train is pictured passing the junction for the former line towards Coldstream. The locomotive was transferred from Tweedmouth to North Blyth during the same month (presumably as a result of the dieselisation of the branch) and would be withdrawn from Tyne Dock the following March, one of 24 of the class to survive into 1967; all would be withdrawn by the end of the year. *Roy Hobbs*

Scotland

Left: Towards the end of their career the five remaining members of the Gresley-designed 'K4' class migrated well away from their traditional West Highland haunts. No 61996 *Lord of the Isles* was reallocated to Thornton Junction in April 1959. Shortly after this transfer, in the same month, the locomotive is seen at Thornton Junction station with a stopping passenger service. It would survive in the Kingdom of Fife until withdrawal in October 1961.
G. H. Hunt/Colour-Rail (Sc917)

Above: Standing outside its new home, Thornton Junction shed, in July 1959 is 'K4' No 61993 *Loch Long*. As LNER No 3441 this was the first of the six-strong 'K4' class to be built, at Darlington Works, in January 1937, the remainder following between then and January 1939; at an average of three 'K4s' per annum, Darlington was not exactly over-exerting itself! As built No 3441 was finished in black, but it was soon to be repainted into standard LNER apple-green passenger livery. The locomotive was transferred from Eastfield to Fife in April 1959, where it was to remain operational for a further 30 months. *C. J. B. Sanderson/Colour-Rail (Sc792)*

Left: The somewhat unorthodox shed allocation painted on the cylinder was more in hope than actuality when this view of 'K4' No 61994 *The Great Marquess* was recorded at Thornton Junction shed in June 1962. By this date No 61994 — the last of its class in service — had been withdrawn for some six months, and it was to remain in store at Thornton Junction for a further two months before being sold for preservation. One of only two LNER 2-6-0s to survive in preservation, as LNER No 3442 this locomotive is currently based on the Severn Valley Railway. *T. B. Owen/Colour-Rail (Sc1247)*

Below: The ex-North British branch to Balloch would eventually be electrified as part of the Glasgow suburban electrification scheme, services being taken over by EMUs in late 1960; the (now closed) section to Balloch Pier followed in 1962. In August 1957 'K2' No 61772 *Loch Lochy* stands in Balloch Central station with a local passenger service. Built in June 1921 as GNR No 1682 by Kitson & Co, the locomotive was by this date allocated to Parkhead, from where it would be withdrawn in November 1959. *D. Eatwell/Colour-Rail (Sc1149)*

Left: In July 1957 'K2/2' No 61775 *Loch Treig* stands in steam at its home shed, Eastfield, with the coaling stage in the background. One of 25 'K2s' built by Kitson & Co, in this case in June 1921, No 61775 would be among the earliest of its class to be withdrawn, succumbing in May 1958. *T. B. Owen/Colour-Rail (Sc403)*

Below: Also seen at its Eastfield home, in October 1960, is 'K2/2' No 61788 *Loch Rannoch*. This locomotive was another constructed by Kitson & Co, as GNR No 1698 in August 1921, and would be the penultimate member of the class to be withdrawn, not being taken out of service (from Eastfield) until June 1961. *C. J. B. Sanderson/Colour-Rail (Sc791)*

Left: In fine external condition, 'K4' No 61995 *Cameron of Lochiel* awaits departure from Crianlarich on 18 June 1960. By this date the 'K4s' had been transferred away from their traditional home on the West Highland line to Thornton Junction, in Fife, where they were to eke out their last years. However, No 61995 returned to the West Highland to provide the motive power for the SLS 'White Cockade' special from Glasgow to Fort William; this was run as part of a week-long tour, organised jointly by the SLS and the RCTS, that also featured some of the famous quartet of restored ScR locomotives. *Derek Penney*

Above: Destination for the SLS-sponsored tour of 18 June was Fort William, No 61995 being seen by the turntable at the shed. The locomotive had been allocated to Eastfield and was thus a familiar sight on the West Highland line until its transfer in December 1959 to Thornton Junction, from where it was withdrawn in October 1961. All five of the 'K4' class were to succumb from Thornton Junction shed between October and December 1961. *Derek Penney*

Left: With No 61995 in the background, 'K1' No 62052, with severely scorched smokebox, is turned on the table at Fort William on 18 June 1960. The 'K1' was allocated to Fort William shed at this time and would remain a West Highland locomotive until its withdrawal in February 1963 as one of the first three of the 70-strong class to be taken out of service. *Derek Penney*

Above: 'K2' No 61794 *Loch Oich* stands outside the shed at Fort William in September 1959. This view shows to good effect the side-window cab fitted to those members of the class transferred north to work on the West Highland line. Allocated to Eastfield at this time, No 61794 would continue to operate over the West Highland line until withdrawal in July 1960. *Malcolm Thompson/Colour-Rail (Sc878)*

A fascinating period scene at Fort William station in August 1959. Alongside the locomotive —'K2/2' No 61787 *Loch Quioch* — can be seen (on the station forecourt) a Morris 8 van belonging to the GPO and an AEC lorry belonging to MacBraynes. The close proximity of the railway line to Loch Linnhe is evident. Today, however, the scene would be radically different; not only are locomotive and vehicles no more, but so too is the station building. In June 1975 the station was relocated slightly to the north, closer to the junction, and the existing site redeveloped. No 61787, another product of Kitson & Co, was by now nearing the end of its career and would remain in service for barely another two months before withdrawal, from Eastfield.
R. E. Toop/Colour-Rail (Sc326)

Right: On 25 May 1961 'K1' No 62052 approaches Fort William station (with the locomotive shed and yard visible in the background) with the 6.30am service from Mallaig. The train would have covered the 42 miles between Mallaig and Fort William in about 90min. *M. Mensing*

Below right: Another view of No 62052 on 25 May 1961, here departing from Fort William with a freight. Until rebuilding of the station at Fort William closer to the junction the line was sandwiched for about a mile between Loch Linnhe and the main A82(T) road. All 70 members of the 'K1' class were still in service at the beginning of 1963, but withdrawals commenced in February, and by the start of the following year 10, including No 62052, had been withdrawn. *M. Mensing*

Left: On 20 May 1961 'K1' No 62034 and 'B1' 4-6-0 No 61342 approach Mallaig Junction, Fort William, with the 1pm service from Mallaig to Glasgow. A Fort William-allocated locomotive throughout the late 1950s, No 62034 was to remain based there until withdrawal in February 1963. *M. Mensing*

Above: 'K1/1' No 61997 *MacCailin Mor* near Glenfinnan with a down freight in April 1961. By now the locomotive was approaching the end of its working career and would be withdrawn barely two months later. It was the only example of the 'K1/1' class, having been rebuilt as a two-cylinder locomotive by Edward Thompson in 1945, effectively as a prototype for the later 'K1' class. The effect of conversion to a two-cylinder design was to reduce, by about 10%, the locomotive's tractive effort. *D. M. C. Hepburne-Scott/Colour-Rail (Sc401)*

It's March 1956, and No 61997 *MacCailin Mor* is seen again amidst the glorious landscape that marks the West Highland line to Mallaig at Glenfinnan with an up service heading towards Fort William. Looking smart in lined black, the locomotive was recently ex-works. At this time it was allocated, appropriately, to Fort William shed (65J), where it would remain until withdrawal in June 1961 — the first of the six locomotives built especially for the West Highland line (albeit rebuilt to 'K1/1') to succumb and the only one not transferred towards the end of its life to Thornton Junction.

J. M. Jarvis/Colour-Rail (Sc108)

Again in March 1956, this evocative scene of a down train departing Glenfinnan for Mallaig features examples of the two classes traditionally associated with the West Highland line — 'K2' No 61791 *Loch Laggan* and 'K4' No 61995 *Cameron of Lochiel* — double-heading the service. At this date the former was allocated to Fort William, from where it would be withdrawn in March 1960, and the latter to Eastfield. Like the other surviving members of the 'K4' class, No 61995 would end its days well away from the splendour of the West Highland line. *J. M. Jarvis/Colour-Rail (Sc737)*

Left: 'K1' No 62052 heads into Lochailort station with the 5.45am service from Glasgow (Queen Street) to Mallaig on 26 May 1961. A Fort William-allocated locomotive, No 62052 would stay on the West Highland line for the remainder of its career. *M. Mensing*

Below: With ex-Caledonian Class 3F 0-6-0 No 57554 in the background, Eastfield-allocated 'K2' No 61788 *Loch Rannoch* stands on shed at Perth in June 1960. By this date the 'K2s' were coming to the end of their long careers; only 10 examples were to survive into the following year, only three in Scotland. No 61788 was one of the last two Scottish examples, eventually being withdrawn in June 1961. *Historical Model Railway Society/Colour-Rail (Sc1245)*

For a period in the early 1950s a number of the Scottish Region 'K2s' were transferred to the Great North of Scotland section, one of which, No 61779, is seen heading an early-morning departure (the 8.11am) from Aberdeen to Ballater in April 1954. The locomotive would remain allocated to Keith for the remainder of its career, being withdrawn from that shed in May 1960. The train is composed of three Gresley coaches, by this time painted in carmine and cream. *J. B. McCann/Colour-Rail (Sc915)*

No 61783 *Loch Sheil* at Craigellachie, Speyside, with a northbound freight heading towards Dufftown and Keith in April 1956. By now allocated to Keith, No 61783 — built by Kitson & Co as one of 25 constructed by that company in 1921 — was one of 20 'K2s' transferred to Scotland between 1925 and 1932 for use primarily on the West Highland line. These locomotives were fitted with side-window cabs, in order to improve conditions for the locomotive crews, as well as deeper ashpans to cope with the Scottish coal, and the 13 examples used chiefly on the West Highland line were named after Scottish lochs. The class continued to operate over West Highland metals until largely displaced by Stanier 'Black Fives'. Withdrawal commenced in early 1957, No 61783 ultimately succumbing (from Keith) in June 1959.
J. B. McCann/Colour-Rail (Sc916)

Looking somewhat careworn, with a well-scorched smokebox door, 'K2' No 61790 *Loch Lomond* was another of the class to venture onto ex-GNSR metals in the twilight of its career, being pictured here blowing off at Keith shed in June 1957, although then allocated to Kittybrewster. *T. B. Owen/Colour-Rail (Sc1246)*

Off the Beaten Track

Although the LMR was to gain an allocation of ex-LNER 2-6-0s when it gained control of the Great Central main line in 1958, occasionally other sections of the LMR witnessed the type in operation. Here 'K3' No 61856 is recorded at Clegg Hall troughs whilst picking up water on a Bradford–Blackpool excursion. Built at Darlington in March 1925, it had been transferred from Annesley (where it had briefly become an LMR locomotive) to Ardsley in May 1959 and would remain allocated to the West Riding shed until withdrawal in December 1962, being one of the last 15 'K3s' to survive; all would be withdrawn by the end of that year. *R. S. Greenwood/Colour-Rail (BRM985)*

Left: In its first years of preservation 'K4' No 3442 *The Great Marquess* visited several parts of the country unfamiliar to the class when in LNER or BR service. On 19 September 1965 the locomotive hauled a circular SLS special from Birmingham. The train's itinerary included a trip up the line from Kidderminster to Alveley Colliery (a route which is nowadays operated by the Severn Valley Railway and on which, ironically, the locomotive is now based), albeit not hauled by the 'K4'. The special is seen departing from Worcester, with the locomotive shed in the background. *Roy Hobbs*

Above: Eighteen months later, on 12 March 1967, No 3442 is seen traversing Southern Region metals at Haywards Heath with a special from Victoria to Southampton and Eastleigh. Amongst other lines visited during this tour were the Lavant and Lymington branches. *Roy Hobbs*

Index of Locations

Full details of Ian Allan Publishing titles can be found on www.ianallanpublishing.com
or by writing for a free copy of our latest catalogue to:
Marketing Dept., Ian Allan Publishing,
Riverdene Business Park,
Molesey Road, Hersham KT12 4RG.

For an unrivalled range of aviation, military, transport and maritime publications, visit our secure on-line bookshop at www.ianallansuperstore.com

or visit the Ian Allan Bookshops in
Birmingham
47 Stephenson Street, B2 4DH;
Tel: 0121 643 2496;
e-mail: bcc@ianallanpublishing.co.uk
Cardiff
31 Royal Arcade, CF10 1AE;
Tel: 02920 390615;
e-mail: cardiff@ianallanpublishing.co.uk
London
45/46 Lower Marsh, Waterloo, SE1 7RG;
Tel: 020 7401 2100;
e-mail: waterloo@ianallanpublishing.co.uk
Manchester
5 Piccadilly Station Approach, M1 2GH; Tel: 0161 237 9840;
e-mail: manchester@ianallanpublishing.co.uk
and (aviation and military titles only) at the
Aviation Experience, Birmingham International Airport
3rd Floor, Main Terminal, B26 3QJ;
Tel: 0121 781 0921
e-mail: bia@ianallanpublishing.co.uk

or through mail order by writing to:
Ian Allan Mail Order Dept.,
4 Watling Drive, Hinckley LE10 3EY.
Tel: 01455 254450.   Fax: 01455 233737.
e-mail: midlandbooks@compuserve.com

You are only a visit away from over 1,000 publishers worldwide.